Poems Promised

Age Cee

BookLeaf Publishing

Presentation by *BookLeaf Publishing*

Web: www.bookleafpub.com

E-mail: info@bookleafpub.com

ISBN : 9789357210027

First edition 2022

DEDICATION

Dedicated to my friends and family. Thank you Rachel for proofreading everything. Thanks to all the others for being inspirations. Rock on.

ACKNOWLEDGEMENT

Much gratitude is given to all who inspired this work - my family, my friends, my dog. And to you my reader, I thank you wholeheartedly, for your support and your time.

PREFACE

Long ago, on a computer far far away, a lowly writer typed out these very words to bare her soul in hopes of creating shared empathetic experiences. Now is where you, the reader, come in - you must use that imagination of yours to see between the lines, hear with the syllables and feel the words jump off the paper. This writer believes in you. Now, you must believe in yourself.

Here's to beginnings

Jovially but
Cautiously caught in the winds
Changing, allons y!

Just wanted to show you

Your eyes
Look but don't see
Your mind, assessing still
Your heart, cold, strong, only glimpsing
Focus

100%

100% Let's go, let's roll, let's see the world
86% Needed to go to the store, brought the dog to enjoy the mode
63% Went to see a friend, trudged through traffic here and then
41% Kind of want to use the sentry, see it all as the car sees
24% Can still make it to and from work, but where is the adapter for a charge?
22% Darkness in the trunk, premature port closure, wait, what, another app?
21% Figured out this station, plugged in with a flick, 90% should do the trick
90% Let's go, let's roll, $11 later, let's see....this world.

Reasons

Rarely do I think of what the world would be without me
Especially since I am thankful for all bestowed upon me
Always striving to do better, be better, better be able to see
Something, a reason for me to go on, to continue to just be
Only when loved ones hurt, painfully, heartbreakingly, unintentionally
New reason must be formed, heartfully, painstakingly.... truly

MOBA!

Ok the time has come to release some stress
Time to play, fight, win, be the best of the best
Pick your fighter, your items, your lane
Team work + good strategy = winning game!
Too many losses are a strain, remember to rest

All the way in CA

When we were young
My sister and I would play
We would talk about
California as being far, far away

On the east coast it was
Just the furthest distance we knew
Farther than any car drive
The most remote on a plane too

On the gulf coast it was
What we saw through the peep hole
Everything looked so teeny tiny
The farthest distance we could behold

Then we were there
In the sun, shine, and splendor
This place didn't seem so distant
This place that we did so adore

Now when we lead our separate lives
Many, many miles apart
We still chuckle and think about CA
Far in distance, close in our hearts

Void

Space, the final frontier
A flight through an endless
Darkness, seeming to expand
Forever.
Curiosity will not kill
A soul here, the abyss beckons
Drawing one silently into its clutches
Closer and closer
Gray to darker gray to an even
Darker gray then BLACK
It's big and frightening
Mysterious
Premonitions are in the air
What will happen here?
In this shadowy eternal chasm where
The words spoken are
In barely a whisper but have an inquiring
Twinge
Leaving is in awe
What has happened here?
And why does it lure
One back…
Into the…
Black.

I, am

I am a hurdle in the last race
I am the slick sai that cuts with a slash
I am the mime that moves, speaking, with a pencil
I am the ninja that shudders to fight
I am the dreaming eyes, the beauty of pupils
I am a doer living for the world
I am an array of ripe stars
I am the clumsy jest
I am the wit of all Junes
I am the stringing of the harp
You see, I am alive, I am alive
I stand in good relation to the earth
I stand in good relation to the moon
I stand in good relation to all that is beautiful
I stand in good relation to the daughter of tern-tainte
You see, I am alive, I am alive

When My Skies are Gray

When my skies are gray
And it's storming, raining too
When it seems like nothing's right
Through the clouds I see you

When my skies are gray
My mood depressed and dreary
I look up and see a friendly face
Standing by me, near me

When my skies are gray
My hourglass on the last grain of sand
I know who I can go to
She is my mother, she understands

I just tell her what is on my mind
I speak to her from my heart
She knows when I am having a bad day
Her words are comforting and smart

When my skies are gray
Though the tempest I see a light
My skies might have just been gray
But my mother is here, I need not fright

Grapes

We are….
Small, oval, squishy and calm
Grouped, clustered together
Purple, green, white and red
A family tree in the flesh
We make…
Juices, sodas, and our cousins,
Raisins. Wines from the finest
Vineyards or just a small snack
Enough to satisfy a sweet tooth
We can…
Bounce roll, fall and decorate
Be eaten, be taken, be bagged
Rhyme with apes, capes and drapes
Hold onto the mother ship until tugged
Away
We are
Many but usually end up as
One small
Snack

Clean or Unseen

You wash your hands every day, I know
Plenty soap and water, not fast, not slow
You scrub and rinse the dirt and scum away
Merrily dry them and go on your way
But what you don't know is what you can't see
Some things so small to eyes of you and me
Evil little germs that have an aim to make you ill
You wash your hands but they cling to you still
The only way to be rid of those little pests
Is to wash your hands, wash them at your best
Not just when you get home from school
But before your eat, don't be a fool
Wash with the best soap, get 'em clean
Between each finger, scrub them, be mean
And when you're done dry the hands with care
Small drops of water could be the bacteria's lair
And one last thing, for I have a job to do
Forget all I just said, so I can infect you!

You'll never Love me

I took a pen and wrote this out
Before it escaped my memory
I wrote this poem just for you
Because I know you'll never like me

I wish that you could see what I do
When I look into your handsome brown eyes
I see someone who I love and care for
Someone I could never despise

Memories come into play here
And I'm remembering very clearly
I have to ask you out on dates
So I know you'll never want me

I know you just want someone else
I just wish that someone was me
What do I lack that she has?
Beauty? Brains? Personality?

I know I like you very much
But reading you is a difficulty
I don't want to ruin our friendship
But I can assume that you'll never need me

You'll never like, want or need

Someone like me to have eternally
I just wish I had the courage to tell you how I
feel
Though sadly I know you'll never have me

Why do I write these heavy love poems
Maybe I should've left it in my memory
My heart aches as I write these last lines
It's a fact now: you will never love me

To Fly

"Flying" above others
Feeling very proud,
Looking down on the lowly,
Mocking their state aloud
Giving those unfortunate ones
Reasons to admire
Talking about the wealthy
The ones "flying" higher
Only few deserve to fly,
Those that help the poor,
Give food to the hungry,
Who give something more
If you get your wings,
And use them at your best,
You will find yourself flying,
Happily with the rest

Leaves

Trees sway
Leaves fall
Breeze blows
Leaves crawl

Feet step,
Leaves crunch
Bags bundle
Leaves bunch

I've got you, little guy

Don't fret, don't cry, don't shed a tear
Just sigh, and relax, and give good cheer
For I've got you, little guy, I got you, bundled in my arms,
I've got you, little guy, I've got you, safe from any harm,
Don't cringe, don't scream, don't yell or shout,
Just smile, and sway and not think to pout,
For I've got you, little guy, I got you, ready to give
I've got you, little guy, I got you, making sure you live
Now lie on my lap, now rest your weary head,
Breathe slowly and soundly, like a picture book being read,
For I've got you, little guy, I got you, now you must rest,
I've got you, little guy, I got you, and am comforting you my best,
The time for bed is growing near, time for young ones to sleep,
Close your eyes tightly now, and count the running sheep,
For I've got you, little guy, I got you, and you're going to be alright,

I’ve got you, little guy, I got you, Goodnight, little guy, Good night.

Light/Dark

Light
Bright, radiance
Dazzling, shining, glowing
Lamps, sunrays, shade, midnight
Scaring, blackening, panicking
Obscurity, shadows
Dark

Tempest Convey

I sprinkle
With soft whispers
Of watered
Gardens and such
I drop
With a SPLAT
Tip-tap, on windows
Dripping is much
I fall
As the wind blows
Together for puddles
Dirt into mud
I pour
Umbrellas!
Windshield-wipers
Ditches flood
I storm
Twisters, cyclones
Thunder, lightning
Hard precipitation
I go
With the cloud
Sun!
Evaporation

Days

Days come, days go
24 hours at all times
Some fast, some slow
I will summarize them with rhyme
When you are waiting
For something to come
The day appears to be fading
It's 3pm, has the day just begun?
Anticipation creeps up upon you
Why can't I have it now?
The day seems to have just dawned on you
Then you get it in the end - wow!
Or when you have a bad spell
You wish you weren't ever born
You tripped on a stone and fell
You anticipate the next morn
The embarrassment seems to last forever
Will it find someone else to bug?
You think: Oh no never
But you cheer up after a hug
When good things arise
Like sports or trips
The days go by
Faster than snow melting on hot lips
And you wonder
Why does the day have to end so soon

You begin to ponder
I thought it was only noon
Days come, days go
24 hours always
Some fast some slow
So how was your day?

Hampered

Gosh I hate
All this smelly
JUNK!
Why don't they
Stuff the trash can
With all this
FUNK!
They hurl
Their clothes in me
Like I don't
CARE!
They think they
Fuss a lot, just wait 'til
I tell them what's not
FAIR!
Do they think
That from all this
I find something to
GAIN?
From all the
constant expansion
Boring on
PAIN?
But would I give
It up, for another
Job?

NEVER!
Heck here's another
Load, this job I'll keep
FOREVER!

Breaking Away

I break tradition
Mistakes outside the line
I can see everything around me
Isn't always what it seems
Not conditioned
To look at my reflection
And not see through the cracks
And to not forget what I'm told
It's all inside my head
I'm so tired of being here
I want to spread my wings
Breakaway from my childish fears
Forsaken
I want to take risks
Have my own opinions
Waste time
I'll do it all
Everything, anything
Just lying here and
Forgetting the world

This isn't the End

A Culmination
A Cessation, but Closure
Here's to Commencement

www.ingramcontent.com/pod-product-compliance
Lightning Source LLC
Chambersburg PA
CBHW051752130826
49812CB00033B/1118
9789357210027